SPOTLIGHT ON CHILDREN'S AUTHORS

LOUIS SACHAR

JOSEPH KAMPFF

Cavendish Square

New York

Published in 2014 by Cavendish Square Publishing, LLC
303 Park Avenue South, Suite 1247, New York, NY 10010

Copyright © 2014 by Cavendish Square Publishing, LLC

First Edition

Website: cavendishsq.com

This publication represents the opinions and views of the author based on his or her personal experience, knowledge, and research. The information in this book serves as a general guide only. The author and publisher have used their best efforts in preparing this book and disclaim liability rising directly or indirectly from the use and application of this book.

CPSIA Compliance Information: Batch #WW14CSQ

All websites were available and accurate when this book was sent to press.

Library of Congress Cataloging-in-Publication Data
Kampff, Joseph.
Louis Sachar / by Joseph Kampff.
p. cm. — (Spotlight on children's authors)
Includes index.
ISBN 978-1-62712-261-0 (hardcover) ISBN 978-1-62712-258-0 (paperback) ISBN 978-1-62712-255-9 (ebook)
1. Sachar, Louis, 1954- — Juvenile literature. 2. Authors, American — 20th century — Biography — Juvenile literature.
3. Children's literature — Authorship — Juvenile literature. I. Kampff, Joseph. II. Title.
PS3569.A226 K36 2014
741.6—d23

Editorial Director: Dean Miller
Senior Editor: Peter Mavrikis
Copy Editor: Cynthia Roby
Art Director: Jeffrey Talbot
Designer: Amy Greenan
Production Manager: Jennifer Ryder-Talbot
Production Editor: Andrew Coddington
Photo research by Julie Alissi, J8 Media

The photographs in this book are used by permission and through the courtesy of: Cover photo by Perry Hagopian; Perry Hagopian, 4; Lisa Romerein/The Image Bank/Getty Images, 6; John-Morgan/Foter/Creative Commons Attribution 2.0 Generic license, 9; Joel Blit/Shutterstock.com, 10; © Scholastic, 12, 17, 18, 22, 23, 27; @ClassicStock/Masterfile, 14; Martin Proll. Houston, Texas/A view across the desert landscape of Big Bend National Park, Texas, 24; Jan Nagle, 27; © Courtesy of Blue Rider Pictures, 28; © AF archive / Alamy, 29; Jan Nagle, 30; courtesy Louis Sachar, 32; courtesy Louis Sachar, 35; Matthew C. Wright/Louis Sachar/http://flickr.com/photos/mattwright/283341191/GNU Free Documentation License, 37.

Printed in the United States of America

CONTENTS

INTRODUCTION:

A Seriously Funny Author

First things first: Louis Sachar's last name rhymes with cracker. Many people know Louis as the author of the bestselling young adult novel *Holes*. People who don't know the novel may know the Disney movie, which is based on the novel and is also called *Holes*. Louis wrote the screenplay for the movie, too. But *Holes* is just one story, and Louis is a man of many stories—some of them told sideways.

Since publishing his first book, *Sideways Stories from Wayside School*, in 1978, Louis has written more than twenty books for kids and young adults. He has a knack for writing about young people. He understands the ways they think, feel, and talk. Louis takes kids very seriously, and he loves writing books about them. His books are wildly imaginative and extremely funny, but they also have a serious side to them—because kids have serious sides.

Louis remembers the orange groves he played in when he was a kid in Tustin. He's sad that they've since been paved over.

Chapter 1
BIRTH! COLLEGE! ELEMENTARY SCHOOL! (IN THAT ORDER)

Louis Sachar was born on March 20, 1954, in East Meadow, New York. His dad, Robert Sachar, was a salesman, and his mom, Ruth Sachar, was a real estate broker. Louis was their second son. He has an older brother named Andy. East Meadow is located on Long Island, New York. When Louis was a kid, his dad worked on the seventy-eighth floor of the Empire State Building. Louis wonders if "maybe that somehow inspired Wayside School, who knows?" When he was nine years old, Louis's family moved from East Meadow to Tustin, California.

Tustin is a city in Orange County, near Los Angeles in southern California. Moving to southern California from Long Island is a big change for a nine-year-old kid. When Louis moved to Tustin there were orange groves everywhere. Louis and his friends used to cut through the groves on the way to school. On their way home, they'd get into orange fights. "The 'ammo' hung from the trees," Louis says, "although the best ones were the gushy, rotten ones on the ground." Tustin has changed a lot since Louis was a kid. He says, "Now, sadly, most of the groves have been paved over and replaced with fast-food restaurants, offices, and housing developments."

Louis was a good student. He went to Barnum Hill School in East Meadow, and Red Hill School in Tustin. He says that "nothing especially traumatic" happened to him in school, but he did have a couple of mean teachers. His fifth grade teacher "always seemed to pick on" him, and his sixth-grade teacher would make the students copy pages from the dictionary when they acted up. Louis remembered this punishment and included it in his book *Sixth Grade Secrets* (1987). But Louis liked school, especially math, and he earned good grades. He fondly remembers his fourth-grade teacher reading E. B. White's *Charlotte's Web* and *Stuart Little* to the class. Louis liked E. B. White because his books were funny and he didn't talk down to his readers. E. B. White later became a big influence on Louis's own writing.

Besides *Charlotte's Web* and *Stuart Little*, Louis wasn't a big fan of children's books when he was a kid. It wasn't until high school that Louis began to love reading. His favorite authors in high school were J. D. Salinger and Kurt Vonnegut. J. D. Salinger's books are meant for older readers and adults, but his books always involve young people. His most famous novel is *The Catcher in the Rye* (1951). Kurt Vonnegut wrote *Cat's Cradle* (1963), *Slaughterhouse-Five* (1969), and *Breakfast of Champions* (1973). Louis says that Salinger, Vonnegut, William Saroyan, and E. L. Doctorow are the authors who most influenced his writing. In high school, Louis wrote a short story called "Apple Power" about a teacher named

Louis studied economics at UC Berkeley, but his favorite college class was at Hillside Elementary School.

Mrs. Gorf who turned her students into apples. His teacher thought Louis hadn't taken the assignment seriously. She did not like the story.

After he graduated from high school, Louis left sunny California for Yellow Springs, Ohio, where he enrolled at Antioch College. Louis didn't stay at Antioch for long. His dad died during his first semester, and Louis went back to California to be with his mom. Back in California, Louis worked for three months as a door-to-door salesman for the Fuller Brush Company, which makes cleaning supplies, brooms, and brushes. "I was great at it," Louis remembers. "My employers couldn't understand why I would want to go back to college when I had such a great career ahead of me selling brushes." This time, Louis decided to stay in California for college. He went to the University of California at Berkeley. Although he majored in

The kids at Hillside loved
Louis. They called him "Louis
the Yard Teacher."

economics and took some creative writing classes, Louis's favorite class in college was working as a teacher's aide at an elementary school.

Louis was on the campus of his college one day when he saw an elementary school girl passing out flyers. Her school was looking for college students to work as teacher's aides in exchange for college credit. This was a deal Louis couldn't pass up: "College credits, no homework, no term papers, no tests—all I had to do was help out in a second/third grade class at Hillside Elementary School." In addition to working in the classroom, Louis became the noontime supervisor, and the kids called him "Louis the Yard Teacher." The kids at Hillside Elementary liked Louis's story about Mrs. Gorf a lot.

Louis's first book, *Sideways Stories from Wayside School*, was inspired by the kids he knew at Hillside.

Chapter 2
LOUIS THE YARD TEACHER... THE LAWYER... THE WRITER

Before working at Hillside, Louis never considered writing children's books for a living. After graduating from college, Louis decided to write *Sideways Stories from Wayside School*. He worked during the day at a sweater factory and wrote the book when he got home at night. *Sideways Stories* is a collection of zany stories about the kids who attend a school that is thirty stories high, with one classroom on each floor. The shortest chapter in the book is the nineteenth story, about a teacher named Miss Zarves. The chapter reads: "There is no Miss Zarves. There is no nineteenth story. Sorry." Louis used his experiences at Hillside to create all the characters in the book. Mrs. Gorf appears in the book as the meanest teacher in the school. Louis also put himself in the book as Louis the Yard Teacher.

After writing *Sideways Stories*, Louis was unsure about what to do next. Even though he decided to go to law school, he still wanted to get his book published. He sent out applications to law schools at the same time as he sent out copies of his manuscript to publishers. *Sideways Stories* was accepted for publication in 1978, during Louis's first semester at Hastings College of the Law. The book was not widely distributed, but the kids who could get their hands on it really liked it. Louis soon began getting fan mail—"tons of it"—from people asking where they could find a copy of the book. The book was popular with students and teachers, but there were not many copies in print, and Louis was unable to support himself by writing.

Louis receives "tons" of mail from his fans. It may take him a while to respond, but he answers every letter.

Louis graduated from law school in 1980. After passing the bar exam, Louis was able to make money practicing law. But all he really wanted to do was to write children's books for a living. He compromised by writing part-time and working part-time at a law firm. He wrote in the morning and practiced law in the afternoon until he was able to earn enough money writing books. When Louis met his wife, Carla Askew, he'd already published two books and was working on his first court case.

Louis and Carla were married in 1985. Carla says that she learned right away that Louis was a writer at heart. "Writing is his love," she says. "How unbelievable to have a chance to do something every day that you relish doing." Not long after publishing his fourth book, *There's a Boy in the Girls' Bathroom*, Louis was able to quit his job and write full-time. "He doesn't consider writing 'work,'" Carla explains. Carla always believed that Louis was a great writer, and she never asked him to get a "real" job. She worked as a teacher and school counselor while Louis stayed home to write. When she wasn't teaching, Carla would leave their apartment for a few hours each morning so Louis could have quiet time to write.

There's a Boy in the Girls' Bathroom is about a fifth-grade bully named Bradley Chalkers. Because he was held back a year for getting bad grades, Bradley is the oldest student in the fifth grade. He doesn't have any friends in school, and his life at home is not much better. Bradley's life changes for the better when he becomes friends with a new kid named Jeff Fishkin. He also starts seeing Carla Davis, the new school counselor. Carla listens to Bradley's stories and encourages him to use his imagination in positive ways.

Like the kids in the Wayside School stories, Louis based some of the characters in *There's a Boy in the Girls' Bathroom* on real people. Carla is based on Louis's wife, and the story of Bradley meeting Jeff comes from one of Louis's friends. On his first day of fifth grade at a new school, Louis's friend sat next to an unpopular kid named Donnie. Even the teacher pointed out that no one liked to sit next to Donnie. "So that's how I began the book, Louis explains. "I changed Donnie's name to Bradley and then started making things up about Bradley."

Louis likes to write stories about kids who are underdogs and outcasts. Even though the odds are against them, the characters in his stories manage to overcome their problems in the end. Louis says he didn't have a particular message in mind when he wrote *There's a Boy in the Girls' Bathroom*. He just wanted to tell Bradley's story. He says the story can "help adults recognize that the kids who cause problems are likely to have problems themselves. Kids can reach the same understanding. I think one of the great things about reading is that it helps readers find empathy for other people, even for someone as outwardly awful as Bradley."

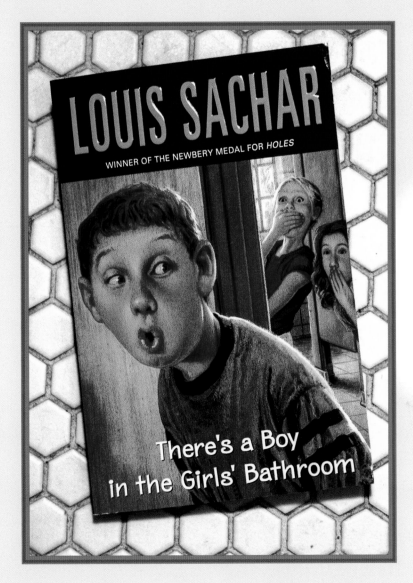

The school counselor in *There's a Boy in the Girls' Bathroom*, Carla Davis, is based on Louis's wife, Carla Askew.

LOUIS SACHAR

WINNER OF THE NEWBERY MEDAL FOR HOLES

The Boy Who Lost His Face

Chapter 3
LOUIS GROWS UP... SORT OF

There's a Boy in the Girls' Bathroom was a major hit for Louis. It was also more serious than the books he had written before. For his next two books, *Sixth Grade Secrets* and *The Boy Who Lost His Face*, Louis continued writing about preteens who face real problems. Writing honestly is important to Louis. He assumes his readers are smart, and he takes them seriously. He says, "I picture my typical reader as reluctant to be taken in by the story, as someone who is very critical and who would see through anything if I tried to trick them. So, I try never to be gimmicky."

Far from "gimmicky," *The Boy Who Lost His Face* was Sachar's most mature novel when it was published in 1989. It's about a boy named David Ballinger who wants to be part of the popular crowd. To try to fit in, he helps a group of kids attack an old woman, Mrs. Bayfield, who the kids accuse of being a witch who steals people's faces. David steals Mrs. Bayfield's cane from her, and she puts a curse on him during the attack. David doesn't take the curse seriously until bizarre things start happening to him. Afraid that he'll have the curse for the rest of his life, David visits Mrs. Bayfield and asks her to lift the curse. He eventually gets Mrs. Bayfield's cane back to her. By the end of the novel, David learns that it is more important to be true to himself than to fit in.

Some people think the language and themes of *The Boy Who Lost His Face* are too mature for a children's book. To honestly portray the lives of his characters, Louis included the curse words that some preteens use. He also put the characters in tough situations. Although Louis's editor approved the manuscript, he was told that one of the words he used may prevent his books from being read by kids. Louis carefully chooses each word in his books, and he was reluctant to change them. He finally agreed to change the language because he knew it wouldn't change the meaning of the story. "As much as I might back down and change a word," he says, "I would never consider altering the moral or political content of a story." Despite the changes Louis made, *The Boy Who Lost His Face* is one of the most often challenged or banned books.

After *The Boy Who Lost His Face*, Louis decided to write a book for his younger fans, who had been asking for new stories from Wayside School. Louis published *Wayside School Is Falling Down* in 1989. That year, Louis also put out a puzzle book called *Sideways Arithmetic from Wayside School*. In the "Yard Teacher's Introduction," Louis explains that he received over ten thousand letters from kids who wanted to go to school at Wayside. Louis, who has always liked puzzles, wrote the book so that kids could see the kind of work the students do there. "It is difficult to explain what sideways arithmetic is," he writes, "I don't understand it too

WHAT IS A CHALLENGED OR BANNED BOOK?

Books are challenged when people or groups try to have them removed from libraries or schools. The books are considered banned if they are actually removed. Parents or organizations may challenge a book if the book goes against their beliefs. Parents usually challenge books that contain words and subjects that they think are not okay for kids. Although many books are challenged in the United States, very few are actually banned. This is because the American Library Association believes that parents should only control their own kids' reading, and that the books in the library should be available to everyone.

Here are some other challenged or banned books you might know:

Harry Potter (series), J. K. Rowling

Goosebumps (series), R. L. Stine

Captain Underpants (series), Dav Pilkey

James and the Giant Peach, Roald Dahl

Louis wrote *Sideways Arithmetic from Wayside School* to show kids what kind of work the kids do at Wayside. Louis loves puzzles.

well, but I'm just the yard teacher. I chase the balls that go over the fence." In fact, Louis understands sideways arithmetic just fine. He invented it!

The book presents a series of problems that seem nonsensical at first. For example, the first question Mrs. Jewels, a popular teacher at Wayside, asks is, "How much is elf plus elf?" The answer, of course, is "fool." This wouldn't make any sense if the book didn't explain step-by-step how to get the answer by substituting numbers for letters in the words. In the first problem $e = 7$, $l = 2$, $f = 1$, and $o = 4$. "They were fun for me to make up," Louis says. "I like doing puzzles of all kinds. It was a real puzzle to make up those problems—as hard as they are to solve, they're even harder to make up."

Louis also created a new series of books about a nine-year-old kid named Marvin Redpost. In the first book, *Marvin Redpost: Kidnapped at Birth?*, Marvin suspects that his mom and dad may not be his real parents because he is the only person in the family with red hair and blue eyes. He becomes convinced that he is really the long-lost son of the King of Shampoon, which would make him a prince. Louis and Carla's daughter, Sherre (pronounced Sherry), was four years old when Louis wrote the first Marvin Redpost book, so he based Marvin's four-year-old sister Lizzie on her. Louis has since written eight Marvin Redpost books. He's also written another book of Sideways arithmetic and a third book of Wayside stories called *Wayside School Gets a Little Stranger*.

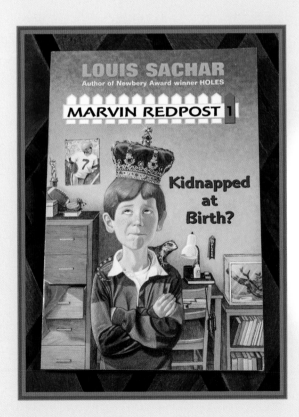

Louis introduced readers to nine-year-old Marvin Redpost in *Marvin Redpost: Kidnapped at Birth?* Marvin has been the subject of eight books to date.

Louis hates hot weather. But the horrible heat of the Texas desert inspired Louis's most famous novel, *Holes*.

Chapter 4
HOLES! THE BIG SCREEN! BRIDGE?

For reasons Louis still doesn't quite understand, the Sachar family moved to Austin, Texas, in 1991. Louis hates the heat. "Anybody who has ever tried to do yard work in Texas in July," says Louis, "can easily imagine hell to be a place where you are required to dig a hole five feet deep and five feet across day after day under the brutal Texas sun." He prefers the cool fog of San Francisco. He also really likes snow, but he wouldn't want to live in a place that snows a lot. Carla says, "I have felt a little guilty for bringing Louis closer to my part of the world—Texas." But moving to Texas may have been the best thing Louis ever did. The unbearable Texas heat inspired *Holes,* the greatest book Louis has written yet.

After finishing *Wayside School Gets a Little Stranger* in 1993, Louis wanted to try writing a novel for adults. He worked on the manuscript for the next two years. In the summer of 1995, the Sachar family went to Maine for vacation—and to escape the summer heat. Louis realized his novel wasn't working out and decided to scrap it. When the family returned to Texas at the end of the summer, it was still very hot outside. Louis closed himself up in his air-conditioned home office and started writing. When interviewers ask him where he got the idea for *Holes*, he says, "From the hot Texas summer."

Louis had already written a bunch of books about kids in school, and he wanted to try something new. *Holes* is about a kid named Stanley Yelnats who is convicted of a crime that he didn't commit. The judge gives him a choice: He could go to jail or he could go to Camp Green Lake. Stanley, who had never been to camp before, chose Camp Green Lake. This turned out to be a big mistake. *Holes* begins: "There is no lake at Camp Green Lake. There was once a very large lake here, the largest lake in Texas. That was over a hundred years ago. Now it is just a dry, flat wasteland." Camp Green Lake is a place where bad boys are sent. Here's the basic idea: "If you take a bad boy and make him dig a hole every day in the hot sun, it will turn him into a good boy." The question is: What are the boys digging for? Louis came up with Camp Green Lake first, and all of the characters and plot came afterward.

Although *Holes* got off to a quick start, Louis took a long time to write the book. Every day, the first thing he would type was the word: "Try." This reminded Louis to keep trying to write a great book, even though he sometimes felt like he was pointlessly digging holes himself. After finishing his fourth draft of the novel, Louis let Sherre read it. She told him which parts she liked best, and which parts she thought needed work. Louis and Sherre also worked on the title together. They almost decided to call the novel *Wrong Place, Wrong Time, Wrong Kid*. Louis took her suggestions and wrote one

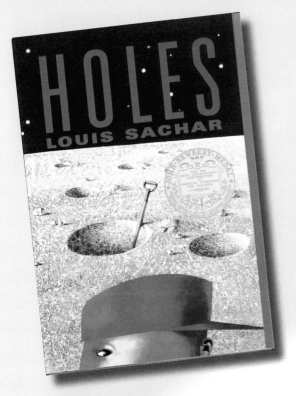

THE JOHN NEWBERY MEDAL

The Newbery Medal is an important award given by the American Library Association for "the most distinguished American children's book." It was the first major award for children's books. The first award was given in 1922. Louis's novel *Holes* won the Newbery Medal in 1999. Here are some other recent Newbery Medal-winning books you might like:

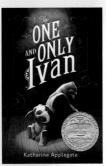

The One and Only Ivan,
Katherine Applegate

Dead End in Norvelt,
Jack Gantos

Moon Over Manifest,
Clare Vanderpool

When You Reach Me,
Rebecca Stead

Louis was heavily involved in the movie adaptation of *Holes*. He wrote the screenplay, and he even visited the set!

more draft before sending it to his publishers.

When Louis began writing *Holes*, he thought he was already as successful as he'd ever be as a writer. But *Holes* was a huge success, and it made Louis more famous than ever. Kids, adults, and critics love the book. Even though *Holes* has mostly boy characters, girls love it too. It's a great book for families to read together. Since it was published in 1998, *Holes* has won several important awards, including the National Book Award and the Newbery Medal.

Disney made *Holes* into a hit movie in 2003. It has also been performed onstage. Louis wrote the screenplay for the movie and the script for the play. At first, Louis wasn't going to write the screenplay. When Louis and the movie director, Andrew Davis, had trouble getting the writer they wanted, Andrew asked Louis to write it. "Well, I don't know how to write a screenplay," Louis said. "Here's my first book being made into a movie, and I want it done right. I'd rather you get someone who really knows what he's doing." Andrew talked him into it, and Louis put as much effort into writing the screenplay as he put into the novel.

Of all the books Louis has written, *Holes* is his favorite. Louis liked the characters in *Holes* so much that he wrote about some of them in *Stanley Yelnats' Survival Guide to Camp Green Lake*

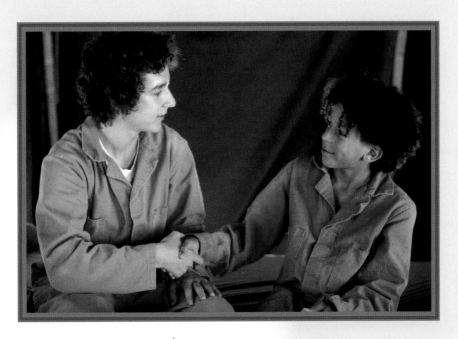

Released in 2003, the movie adaptation of *Holes* proved as popular with kids as the book.

and *Small Steps*. The *Stanley Yelnats' Survival Guide* offers helpful advice for new inmates at Camp Green Lake, like how to dig perfect holes and identify rattlesnakes. *Small Steps* tells the story of Armpit, a former inmate at Camp Green Lake who tries to make a better life for himself after his release. Unfortunately, trouble (in the form of another former inmate named X-Ray) seems to follow him everywhere.

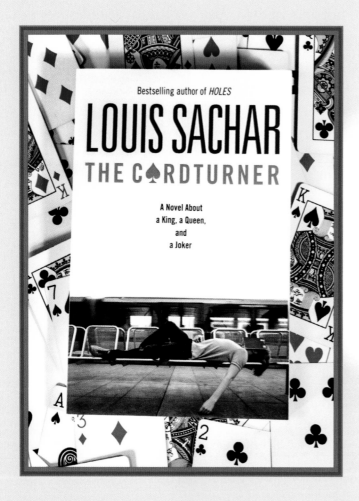

The *Cardturner*, Louis's most recent novel, involves his favorite card game, bridge. Don't be too surprised if you've never heard it. As Louis explains, "the people who play bridge seem to live in their own alien world."

A FEW WORDS ABOUT BRIDGE

Louis says that bridge is "a card game that was once extremely popular but that, unfortunately, not too many people play anymore, especially not young people. In fact, the people who play bridge seem to live in their own alien world." Bridge is a little more complicated than other card games, but that doesn't mean it's impossible to learn. Lately, schools have begun offering bridge programs for kids. Playing bridge helps kids learn to solve problems by thinking critically. In that way, bridge is lot like chess. Bridge is a more social game than chess because it's played in groups.

Louis has also written a young adult novel titled *The Cardturner*. It's about a seventeen-year-old boy named Alton Richards whose great-uncle Lester is old, blind, and very rich. Lester is also one of the best bridge players in the world. Bridge is a complicated card game, and Lester needs someone to drive him to bridge tournaments and read his cards for him. Alton's parents convince him that Lester is dying and that they can get some of his money if Alton takes him to his bridge tournaments. *The Cardturner* has a lot of information about bridge, but the narrator gives his readers the option to skip those parts if they want to.

Louis's daughter Sherre is the first person to read his books when he finishes a draft.

Chapter 5
SO, WHAT'S IT LIKE TO BE A FAMOUS AUTHOR?

According to Louis's older brother Andy, Louis hasn't changed a lot since becoming famous: "He still likes stories, he still likes puzzles, and he still likes his friends." When Louis was six years old, he taught Andy how to play chess. These days Louis likes to play duplicate bridge, and he goes to the local club a few times a week to play. "I've always been a game-player," Louis explains, "and I think bridge is one of the greatest games ever invented. It's too bad that not many young people play it anymore." Louis is a quiet, thoughtful guy. He likes watching baseball, and his favorite team is the San Francisco Giants. He has a mixed-breed dog named Watson.

Sherre says Louis thinks of himself as "a writer and a dad who just happens to have the exact same name." When Sherre was little (she's grown up now and graduated from college at Cornell University), Louis was already finished working for the day and ready to play when she came home from school. In an article she wrote when she was twelve years old, Sherre says: "He likes to challenge me in video games, pinball, and basketball, or to help me with his favorite thing, my math homework." Other kids have always asked Sherre about her dad, especially after Louis read *Holes* to her fifth grade class. She says, "I have . . . learned that I have to share part of my dad with all the other kids in the world. We just love him for two different reasons."

Louis gets a ton of mail. Ever since he published his first book, kids and adults have written to him with interview questions or just to talk about his books. Because he gets so many letters, it can take a long time before he gets a chance to respond. Louis answers every letter he receives from his fans. Carla says, "Most of the letters ask the same questions over and over, year after year, but each child is important to him, so he is determined to give them all the respect they deserve."

It takes Louis about two years to finish a book. He works for about one or two hours every morning. Louis never talks about what he's writing until the book is finished, not even to Carla or Sherre, so there's no telling what he'll come up with next. "When he is first getting started on a new book," Carla says, "we can often hear the rumble of the pinball machine in his office after only an hour or so of work. We're always surprised when he says he's almost finished with a new book. Those few hours a day can really add up to time well spent for his readers." When he finishes a book, Sherre is usually the first to read it.

Writing doesn't always feel like time well spent to Louis. He writes about six drafts of every book, changing things around and making the book better each time. Louis says, "If it's too

Louis's work schedule leaves plenty of time for him and Sherre to watch his favorite baseball team, the San Francisco Giants.

boring for you to want to rewrite, then it's going to be too boring for anyone else to want to read." Most days he feels as if he hasn't achieved much. "It amazes me how after a year, all those wasted days somehow add up to something," Louis says. Louis spends so much time and effort on his books because he believes that an author's first job is to write a great book. Writing a great book is hard work. Coming up with the story and characters and setting is not easy. Louis gets writer's block a lot, and he says it's not much fun when he doesn't know what to write. But in the end, all of the hard work is worth it. "I'm proud of each and every one of my books," says Louis. "I think that nothing else comes close to that."

Although it's hard work,
Louis loves writing
books for a living.
He's always smiling!

BOOKS BY LOUIS SACHAR

Wayside Books

Sideways Stories from Wayside School

Wayside School Is Falling Down

Sideways Arithmetic from Wayside School

More Sideways Arithmetic from Wayside School

Wayside School Gets a Little Stranger

Marvin Redpost Books

Marvin Redpost: Kidnapped at Birth?

Marvin Redpost: Why Pick on Me?

Marvin Redpost: Is He a Girl?

Marvin Redpost: Alone in His Teacher's House

Marvin Redpost: A Flying Birthday Cake?

Marvin Redpost: Class President

Marvin Redpost: A Magic Crystal?

Marvin Redpost: Super Fast, Out of Control!

Other Books by Louis Sachar

Johnny's in the Basement

Someday Angeline

There's a Boy in the Girls' Bathroom

Sixth Grade Secrets

The Boy Who Lost His Face

Dogs Don't Tell Jokes

Monkey Soup

Holes

Stanley Yelnats' Survival Guide to Camp Green Lake

Small Steps

The Cardturner

AUTHORS LOUIS SACHAR LIKES TO READ

Margaret Atwood
Avi
E. L. Doctorow
William Goldman
Lois Lowry
Walter Dean Myers
Katherine Paterson
Richard Price
J. D. Salinger
William Saroyan
William Sleator
Kurt Vonnegut
E. B. White

GLOSSARY

Louis writes books for kids, but that doesn't mean he only uses words kids know. "I never simplify," he says. "I don't constrict my vocabulary. If a reader doesn't know the meaning of a word, he can look it up."

banned–when a book, movie, or other kind of artwork is not allowed to be read or seen

bar exam–the test people have to pass to work as lawyers

college credit–work that counts toward a college degree

critic–a person whose job is to judge and comment on books, movies, or other kinds of art

housing development–an area where new houses are built

majored–focused on a particular subject in school

manuscript–the original copy of an author's work

political content–social themes in a book, movie, or other kind of artwork

publication–when a book is released to be sold to the public

real estate broker–a person who helps people buy and sell property

screenplay–a script used to make a movie

semester–part of a school year; colleges usually have a spring and a fall semester

writer's block–when an author cannot figure out what to write

CHRONOLOGY

March 20, 1954: Louis Sachar is born in East Meadow, New York.

1963: Louis's family moves to Tustin, California.

1972: Louis goes to Antioch College in Ohio, but returns to California in his freshman year after his father dies.

1975: Louis works as a teacher's aide at Hillside Elementary School.

1976: Louis graduates from University of California, Berkeley with a bachelor's degree in economics.

1978: Louis publishes *Sideways Stories from Wayside School*. He begins law school at Hastings College of Law in San Francisco.

1980: Louis graduates from law school at Hastings College of the Law in San Francisco.

1985: Louis marries Carla Askew.

1987: Louis publishes one of his most popular books, *There's a Boy in the Girls' Bathroom*. Louis and Carla's daughter, Sherre, is born.

1989: Louis's books sell well enough that he is able to stop practicing law and focus on writing full-time.

1991: Louis and his family move to Austin, Texas.

1998: Louis publishes *Holes*; wins the National Book Award.

2003: The Disney movie *Holes* appears in theaters.

2010: Louis publishes *The Cardturner*.

FURTHER INFORMATION

Books

If you love reading stories and want to learn how to write your own, these books can help:

Levine, Gail Carson. *Writing Magic*. New York: Collins, 2006.

Messner, Kate. *Real Revision: Authors' Strategies to Share with Student Writers*. Portland, ME: Stenhouse, 2011.

Websites

Louis Sachar's Official Website

www.louissachar.com

Louis's website includes a frequently asked questions (FAQ) section in which Louis answers the questions he most often receives from teachers and kids. The website also has a list of all of his books, a short biography of Louis, and a question and answer (Q&A) page about *Holes*.

BIBLIOGRAPHY

ONLINE SOURCES

"Banned & challenged books." American Library Association. http://www.ala.
   org/advocacy/banned, May 11, 2009.

Compton's by Britannica, Encyclopædia Britannica Online School Edition. s.v.
   "Sachar, Louis." http://school.eb.com/comptons/article-9343959, 2013.

Contemporary Authors Online. s.v. "Louis Sachar." 2009.

Davis, Kate. "A Conversation with Louis Sachar." 2002. Writing 25, no. 3
   (2002): Academic Search Complete.

Fust, Julia. 2006. "An Interview with Louis Sachar." *New York Times*, January
   15. http://www.nytimes.com/2006/01/15/books/review/sachar-interview.
   html.

Hearne, Betsey. 1998. "He Didn't Do It." *New York Times*, November 15. http://
   www.nytimes.com/books/98/11/15/reviews/981115.15
   hearnet.html.

Hu, Winnie. 2011. "For Students Raised on iPods, Lessons in Bridge." *New
   York Times*, April 24.

Kenower, Bill. "Louis Sachar Interview." Author magazine video, 6:21. https://
   www.youtube.com/watch?v=7vUpO5cgZ1w.

Louis Sachar's website, http://www.louissachar.com, 2002.

Random House Kids. "Louis Sachar Classroom Cast." Random Books video,
   4:35. https://www.youtube.com/watch?v=3y-hfPPPl9E.

Reynolds, Susan Salter. 2003. "Louis Sachar's Odyssey." *Los Angeles Times*,
   January 5. http://articles.latimes.com/2003/jan/05/magazine/tm-sachar1.

"The John Newbery Medal," American Library Association. http://www.ala.org/alsc/awardsgrants/bookmedia/newberymedal/aboutnewbery/aboutnewbery.

BOOKS

Greene, Meg. *Louis Sachar*. New York: Rosen Central, 2004.

Sachar, Andy. "Louis Sachar Takes Long Walks with His Dog Every Morning." *Holes*, 10th Anniversary Edition. New York: Farrar, Straus and Giroux, 2008. 237–243.

Sachar, Carla. "A Writer or a Lawyer?" *Holes*, 10th Anniversary Edition. New York: Farrar, Straus and Giroux, 2008. 248–251.

Sachar, Louis. *Holes*, 10th Anniversary Edition. New York: Farrar, Straus and Giroux, 2008.

___. "Newberry Medal Acceptance." *Holes*, 10th Anniversary Edition. New York: Farrar, Straus and Giroux, 2008. 252–264.

___. *The Cardturner*. New York: Ember, 2010.

___. *Sideways Arithmetic from Wayside School*. New York: Scholastic, 1989.

___. *Sideways Stories from Wayside School*. New York: Harper Trophy, 2003.

Sachar, Sherre. "Are You Really Louis Sachar's Daughter?" *Holes*, 10th Anniversary Edition. New York: Farrar, Straus and Giroux, 2008. 244–247.

Smith, Evan. "Louis Sachar." *Texas Monthly*. January 2006. 94–102.

INDEX

ABOUT THE AUTHOR:

Joseph Kampff is a lifelong student of literature. He's been a fan of Louis Sachar's books ever since he discovered *Sideways Stories* in the school library when he was in the third grade. He loves reading Louis's books to his own kids, and he hopes you'll love reading them, too. Joseph lives in Brooklyn, NY, with his wonderful family and their dog, Sadie-Belle. He loves reading, but he doesn't have the brains for sideways arithmetic.